PSAD

Post Service Adjustment Disorder

Archway Publishing books may be ordered through booksellers or by contacting:

Archway Publishing
1663 Liberty Drive
Bloomington, IN 47403
www.archwaypublishing.com
1 (888) 242-5904

Because of the dynamic nature of the Internet, any web addresses or
links contained in this book may have changed since publication and
may no longer be valid. The views expressed in this work are solely those
of the author and do not necessarily reflect the views of the publisher,
and the publisher hereby disclaims any responsibility for them.

Any people depicted in stock imagery provided by Getty Images are
models, and such images are being used for illustrative purposes only.
Certain stock imagery © Getty Images.

This book is a work of non-fiction. Unless otherwise noted, the author
and the publisher make no explicit guarantees as to the accuracy of
the information contained in this book and in some cases, names of
people and places have been altered to protect their privacy.

ISBN: 978-1-4808-6092-6 (sc)
ISBN: 978-1-4808-6091-9 (hc)
ISBN: 978-1-4808-6093-3 (e)

Library of Congress Control Number: 2018945121

Print information available on the last page.

Archway Publishing rev. date: 5/25/2018

ACKNOWLEDGMENTS

All artwork and cover design created by:
Patrick King
www.patrickkingart.com
Editor:
Dr. Kevin B. Vichcales
Back Cover Photography: Art Rodriguez

Special thanks to the following people for your support, inspiration, critique, and input along the way: James "Frosty" Carmichael, Cliffton "The Cliffman" Elliott, Travis "The Travman" Roha, Michael Plover, Hunter Alexander "Cazadore" Haley, Justin "The Juice" Downey, Speedy Hart, Tom Woodley, Sarah Jane Samuels, Jose Ortiz, Emily Robbins, Nelson Canales, Lee de Luna, Michelle Washington, Miguel Ybarra, Ph.D., Ed Wimpy, James Michael Tello, Terry Rolen, David Polin, Javier Perales, and Father Peter McKenna.

I especially would like to thank God the Father in Heaven for the gifts of humility and vision through all the years of trials and tribulations.

All definitions for the diagnoses of veterans that are in this book were paraphrased from the Diagnostical and Statistical Manual or DSM 5—2013 edition, National Institute for Mental Health (NIMH) and other various mental health resources. The DSM-5 is developed and researched by the American Psychological Association.

Statistics on Veteran homelessness, substance abuse, suicide rates and other ailments can be found at www.va.gov and at www.census.gov

Any and all inquiries, perspectives and input from you, the reader, can be submitted via email at: input@psad03.com

CONTENTS

A MESSAGE TO SERVICE MEMBERS AND VETERANS

This book is for you. I am no expert. I am neither a Ph.D. nor psychologist—at least not yet- maybe one day. I am one of you. Like you, I enlisted into the Armed Forces with a desire to serve my country. We all served our country in our own way, whether it was Air Force, Army, Navy, or Marines. We are all people who joined the military looking to broaden our understanding of the world and take our lives to the next level. Maybe we were not ready for college. Perhaps we never saw ourselves going to college. Possibly we liked the benefits or it was a dream when we were very young. Maybe there was some family history of military service and it was our turn to carry the torch. For some of us, it could have been that we needed a challenge. And maybe—just maybe—we were doing absolutely nothing with our lives after high school except getting into trouble and needed a change. Whatever the reason, we joined, and that alone says a lot about you and me.

Some of you who read this may at first perceive this as whining and complaining, and back on base, that's exactly what this is. Some of you may say," Suck it up Marine !!" That's cool. However, I am willing to bet that perhaps some of you are neck deep in what I am talking about and completely oblivious or too proud to admit that life is pretty rough. "Shit-bags can't carry their own weight" was my mentality too. I was built for the military life, just like many of you. But bring that attitude back home to the civilian world, and watch life totally kick the ever-living crap out of you.

Really think about it. Are you honestly happy where you are at? I'm expecting some serious backlash from some of you, but with so many veterans killing themselves on a daily basis, I know a problem exists, and I am choosing to address it.

Some of us did very well in our Enlistments/Commissions and some of us did not. That does not mean you and I are not allowed to have a good life after taking the oath. But how exactly do we do that? How do we take what we have learned and make it into an asset for us in the civilian world? It is a very real challenge for a lot of us, and it is also very easy to blame civilians for why some of our lives spun way off track when we got home. That is what we have been doing for far too long, and getting us absolutely nowhere. We need to stop blaming them. We need to stop blaming the world around us. It is not all their fault, and we need to own this epidemic of veteran failure. Granted, there are so many people who disrespect us and really don't care what we have seen or done while in service. But an even greater number of people *do* care. They want to help, try to help, and give all they can to help and cannot seem to get through.

Country stars, rock bands, hip-hop/R&B artists, celebrities, employment companies, schools, teachers, private citizens, doctors, counselors, social workers, family, and friends throughout the globe all give a great deal of what they can for us. But we cannot put the entire weight of our problems on them and expect to make the changes we need to make within ourselves. As difficult as it was to do what we did, I am sorry to say that the fight isn't over just because we are not in uniform anymore.

Perhaps some of you are so ashamed and broken to even think about reaching out for help. You keep trying to convince yourself that you can figure this out on your own. Maybe you feel like you've disgraced yourself and your brothers and sisters in arms and have lost all your honor. Worst of all, perhaps you just don't give a shit anymore about anything or anyone—including yourself.

When you do finally find the guts to reach out, all you have is a

1-800 number, an email address, and/or maybe a Web page. I know your pain. Truly I do. I personally had no idea how hard the fight was going to be when I got home. It completely broadsided me and took me down such an incredibly dark path that I could not get out on my own. Through the Grace of God and my family who refused to give up on me, even when I gave up on myself, I got out of that mess. It was the hardest thing I ever did. It was literally a hundred times harder than scaling Recon Hill, Sheep Shit, Buddha, Ball Buster, and Mount Motherfucker (to all my Horno and San Mateo dogs) all in one day, and I know I'm one of the lucky ones. But I don't have to be. Perhaps by thinking about this you can see that there is a way out.

Some of the illustrations and examples in these writings are based from an Infantry Marine's point of view simply because that is what I saw and experienced. Other examples are from testimonies and observations from hundreds of veterans over the years. Each one of you has your own story and your own path that led you to where you are at this very moment. What is most important to remember is that I am not alone. And neither are you. Maybe you can relate to some of this, perhaps you can relate to none of this, and just maybe you can relate to all of this.

I did not see combat. My end of active service (EAS) was August 2001; therefore, I had to watch everything from the sidelines. However, I also saw that a lot of struggles from both non-combat and combat veterans were very similar to mine, especially when they came home. On top of that, I've had people flat-out come and tell me that, because I did not see combat, I do not deserve the benefits of those who did and neither do you. I don't pay attention to that ignorance, and even the best medicine will never cure stupid. But I do see a hard level of disconnect from civilians and service members, and perhaps Post Service Adjustment Disorder (PSAD) is why.

Those of you out there who have seen combat, who went over there and kicked some serious ass and are struggling with hard times, broken bodies and/or PTSD, know this: *you* are my hero. I am praying for you every day, and so many other great people are doing the same. I would have fought right alongside you, but my time and my fight were not there with you. God Bless all of you who gave all you had over there and all those who paid the ultimate sacrifice.

If you were one of the ones to come home and easily transition right into civilian life, I hope you realize how truly blessed and fortunate you were. The number of veterans who can flow that smoothly out of service is far lower than that of those who stumble and fall. Maybe you can help teach those who are struggling a thing or two on how to do it.

It truly is an unfortunate thing that happens to a lot of us when we get out. We come home excited and ready to take on the world. We return to our families and homes with a drive to move our lives forward. It feels good for a while. Everyone is happy to see you. You've earned some bragging rights in one way or another, and you were really good at what you did. Even if you were a shit-bag and just did what you had to in order to finish your contract, you were probably just as excited as I was to come home.

Then something really weird starts to happen. Everything you thought would happen when you got out doesn't quite take shape. You find yourself in a place where things don't feel the same. You become disoriented and discouraged little by little because it really feels like people around you start to let you down. They don't respond the same way your buddies did while you were in. You start to feel like an oddball because the world around you just does not understand you anymore or make any sense. You go from hero to zero within a short period of time.

I ask you to read this with an open heart and an open mind. Take your time and think about your life. Perhaps you are in that place right now, where the harder you try to make civilian life work for you, the more it crashes and burns in absolute failure. If you can relate to any of this, then perhaps you also can help save your own life and another veteran's. PSAD is a concept that derives from over ten years of my own personal experience and from countless stories like yours that veterans, willing to describe their experiences, shared with me. Perhaps what we needed was a perspective of what's wrong from within our own ranks. This is an attempt to give exactly that.

Currently in this country, everyone is pointing fingers at everyone. It's the government's fault. It's the president's fault. It's the VA's fault. It's the Republicans. It's the Democrats. It's the civilians. It's the wars we've fought. If you were hoping for a book that points a finger at anyone, then you might as well move on because that is not what this is about. This is an objective look at the different lenses that military and civilians look through that blinds both sides and can cause so much devastation for veterans and their families. The bottom line is that I'm calling everyone out on this one—both veterans and civilians.

What's important to me is that I want to help fight the good fight. As of 2017, we're losing roughly five thousand veterans a year to suicide alone. Honorably discharged veterans are being sent to prison for crimes they have committed, drug rehabs are packed, and the homeless rates are skyrocketing out of control. That shit has got to stop. Something has to change. Join me and fight the good fight.

Respectfully from your brother,

Cpl. Valdez

United States Marine Corps

2/1 Echo Company, 3rd Platoon, 97-01

PREFACE

For My Dear Son Sean

My son, Sean McGrew, served in the United States Marine Corps for four years as an 0311 Infantryman and was Honorably Discharged in late 2001. When he came home, he tried several careers after the Marine Corps to include automotive engineering. He later became a firefighter/paramedic in the Dallas area of Texas. He took his own life on April 13, 2012, at the age of thirty-three.

It wasn't until I lost him that I found out from his friends and coworkers just what a wonderful person people thought he was. I always knew it myself, but to hear it from so many other people who truly cared for him really made it that much harder for me to deal with. Unfortunately for Sean, he himself did not realize how special he was to so many.

Sean always had a hard time fitting in. He wasn't a troubled teen in the traditional sense (drugs, alcohol, getting into trouble with the law, and so on), but he just didn't like to follow the crowd. He preferred to make his own rules and decisions that would sometimes get him into trouble. His father and I encouraged him to join the Armed Forces thinking it would give him the discipline he lacked and hopefully put him on a path that would help him have a better life. Little did I know, it would lead to his demise.

After reading Danny's book (the one you're about to read), I saw Sean virtually on each and every page. At family gatherings after Sean was discharged, he always seemed to be uneasy. He would leave early.

He would say things that we wouldn't understand, or would become impatient. A lot of times, he would just sit there with a strange look on his face. He just didn't fit in. On the surface, he always seemed to be happier with his buddies than with the family, but personally I knew that his family meant more to him than the world. He would tell that to me all the time. His actions, however, would confuse the family around him and sometimes would cause a lot of frustration for everyone. People would say, "It's just Sean being Sean." But now in retrospect, I think it was something different. I think it was something deeper.

I believe Danny is onto something here. I believe this concept of PSAD needs to be investigated further. We are losing our servicemen and women at alarming rates. Not one single parent needs to experience what I have been through. Something must be done for Sean's sake … for all of our sakes.

Debbie Nicholson
Proud Mother of Sean Michael McGrew

THE CONCEPT

WHAT YOU ARE ABOUT to read is a collaboration of four years of service in the United States Marine Corps (USMC) followed by over fifteen years of collecting and recording various forms of testimonies, interviews, therapy, counseling, group discussions, rehabilitation, recovery, Ministry work and Faith-based retreats. I have spent countless hours working with veterans as a volunteer, observing patterns and behaviors, and listening to their stories, along with recording and documenting my own personal experiences. I have taken those fifteen years' worth of stories, notes, and data, put them into chronological order, summarized them and gave them a name. The end result was this concept of Post Service Adjustment Disorder or PSAD. Probably the hardest part of all of this was listening to the mothers of my fellow Devil Dogs and service members who took their own lives. If it were that hard for me to hear it, I can only imagine how hard it was for them to tell it.

In this book, we will analyze and attempt to understand the very concept of PSAD. By giving it a name, we have identified the problem and once it has been identified, we can begin to formulate solutions. Ultimately the end result I am hoping for is to help put an end to all of the unfortunate tragedies and despair that happen to so many great veterans and their families.

Over the years, literature on PTSD or Post Traumatic Stress

Disorder, has been further developed and generally describes the condition as deriving from a life-altering event that a person can experience. In most common situations, the person is threatened in some way or has seen some god-awful thing or event with the end result of flashbacks, nightmares, and impulsive, self-destructive behavior. While there is no doubt this is a very real element of what makes PTSD, there is another aspect that has only begun to be addressed or developed.

In recent years, there are studies being conducted that have identified military transition and adjustment to civilian culture as a key component to veteran struggle. I am a firm believer that *every* veteran will face PSAD in one way or another and on many different levels of severity from very mild all the way up to severe.

PSAD can be defined as the complete mental breakdown and incompatibility, both consciously and subconsciously, of a military service member during transition back to civilian culture. Take note. Not one time throughout the following text is there ever mentioned stories of dead bodies, violent missions, horrific imagery, and traumatic situations. There is a big difference between PTSD and PSAD and understanding those differences is paramount to enable smoother transition for outgoing military personnel and their families.

After researching the internet, the DSM-5, the ICD-10, and other mental health resources, the only diagnosis that comes even remotely close is called adjustment disorder, which until recently has gained little traction amongst researchers across the globe. Considering that suicide rates are roughly up to five thousand veterans annually, it is reasonable to suggest that we need a different approach.

From a personal viewpoint, my experience with transition from military to civilian and the mental illnesses that were diagnosed had always felt a little off target and did not quite seem to make sense to me. After communicating with and observing many fellow Devil Dogs and veterans from around the globe, I am finding more and more similarities in this form of an adjustment issue or PSAD.

It was *not* trauma for many service members, myself included. It was an absolute love of the job, The Corps, and service to each other and our country. It was a lifestyle that was filled with intensity, integrity, dark humor, honor, code, and countless other awesome memories. The beans, bruises, beers, bullets, bangs, and broken bones were all part of the job. Period. And for almost all of us, it was the same mentality. It was all we knew. It was the way we knew how to get things done. How to fight, excel, laugh, eat, work, play, and socialize. In the military, that way of life fits perfectly in that setting. However, pretty much all of that military work ethic and code of conduct does not translate well with the civilian world. From my personal experience, I had no idea why over time I was becoming increasingly isolated from friends and family due to my Marine way of doing things.

I therefore advocate that more research and development is needed on PSAD so that gainful transitional programs can be revised and developed to better help veterans.

In the following chapters, I have broken down, step by step, the journey a person can take from high school all the way to a veteran struggling with PSAD. Some of these steps are very elementary and obvious; however, I do feel the need to include them as they are still a part of the journey that many veterans undertake. I have noticed that a lot of times, simple little things like what happens to a person after high school and how an individual ends up in basic training get overlooked. Yet, in my opinion, they are still contributing variables to the end result of a veteran in despair. A lot of the illustrations and examples were part of my everyday life as a United States Marine.

A FORK IN THE ROAD

CIVILIAN CULTURE IS QUITE a challenge for young adults all on its own. After high school, choices must be made to enable the individual to gain his or her own independence and financial stability. Hopping from job to job can happen as the individual experiments with different employment opportunities and careers. If a young adult is really locked on with discipline and responsibility, he or she begins to learn right away the importance of a good budget to allow for a social life as well as meeting his or her basic needs such as rent, groceries, car payments, and utilities. If these individuals do not learn the importance of good budgeting, they can crash and burn very easily by having their car repossessed and the lights shut off at home. They can end up living on Ramen noodles and, of course if things get way out of control, have to move back home with family members.

All of that decision making and learning is centered around a lot of trial and error. A young adult may have an idea about a good career endeavor, but after pursuing that career, may find hard truths that make him or her reconsider. That's where "learning experiences" teach that individual a lot about the world around him or her. Perhaps the pay wasn't as good as the person thought or the hours didn't work for that individual. Maybe the job required a lot of internal discipline that perhaps that individual was not ready to undertake. No matter the case, he or she can easily decide to abandon that endeavor and pursue something else.

College or technical education is another direction within civilian culture that many young adults may decide to pursue. Only this time, they are given their freedom to make their own decisions. They have to make the choice whether to go to class or not. They can determine whether to study or not. They can decide which degree option entices them the most and how to develop good study habits and social settings.

With similarities to a non-college young adult, a lot of trial and error is occurring. Hanging out the night before a big test and partying at all hours might not be such a good idea after a couple of poor grades surface. Disconnecting from individuals who have different priorities, even though they are good "friends," may be needed in order to maintain forward progression. Learning to use good discipline and turning in high-quality work can teach the individual that hard work pays off with benefits of scholarships, teacher praise, and career opportunities.

The civilian world moves at its own pace. For the most part, it works from eight to five, Monday through Friday. It has its own medical care, law enforcement, economic structure, and judicial system. It can be described as a very grey, multileveled environment. Bad choices and failures can be repaired. There's always room for a second chance and a third and a fourth or until the world works for that particular individual. A person can decide one day that he or she doesn't want to live in California and move to Texas, New York, or any other destination. The purpose in life for civilians can change at any given moment, and there is freedom to make that change a reality. One day they may be dedicated to the medical field, and the next, they find themselves in the legal world or engineering. The road for any young adult is wide open, filled with ups and downs, challenges, failures, successes, trial and error, and, of course, choices to do whatever they want.

A lot of times, however, high school graduates may find themselves in an aimless situation. They did not have neither the grades nor drive to want to go to college; therefore, future preparations such as college applications, university shopping, or professional degree options were not pursued. Given the state of the present economy, it is fair to say that, if there were intentions to pursue a degree, they were put on the back burner due to financial limitations.

The military can be a great option for many young adults who are in that situation to help with direction and guidance. It can be an excellent opportunity to be a part of something bigger and to learn and see for themselves the truths about the world. Add to that college benefits and many other perks for serving in the military, enlisting or gaining a Commission can be a great "next step" to progress their young adult lives forward. But what is unknown or sometimes overlooked is that individual has chosen a path at a fork in the road of their lives. As a result, that decision will take him or her on a life journey that is a completely different lifestyle and culture outside of being a civilian.

It is important to note that each branch of the Armed Forces has a different way of doing things. The levels of intensity, discipline, amplitude, and troop interaction, for the most part, all differ from each other. However, after communicating with many social workers and therapists who deal with veterans from all branches on a daily basis, there are strong similarities of adjustment problems caused by the differences between civilians and military personnel in general.

I served in the United States Marine Corps, and these were the experiences I personally witnessed both while serving and upon my return home. The objective here in the following chapters is to demonstrate military language, culture, and daily interaction, so feel free to recall your own personal experiences.

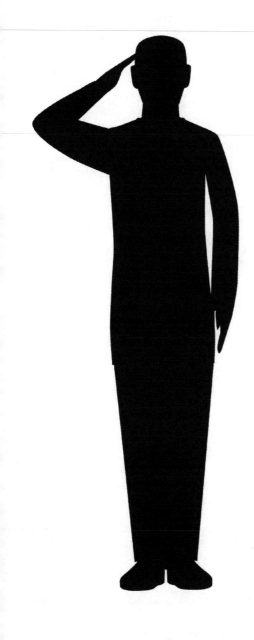

THE LIFE

FROM THE MOMENT a person is taken off the civilian bus and flung into boot camp mode, a massive overload of culture shock is instilled. The yelling, the speed necessary to complete the tasks given by the drill instructors, the obedience to orders, and the utmost discipline of the mind and body is all amped up to a very high level. Conformity to this way of life is essential to surviving boot camp. And more importantly, to excel in boot camp, conformity must be adapted rather quickly by each individual in order to earn the title of United States Marine.

The men and women who cannot or will not adapt to that way of life are washed out of service and sent home. All others go on to serve in one of the most elite fighting branches of the Armed Forces. All of that amplitude has a place and a purpose in an entity like the Marine Corps. The laughs and pain shared amongst fellow platoon members help create a solid bond of brotherhood and sisterhood. It is the ultimate goal that is desired, and recruits are proud to earn it. The leaders that emerge from those ninety days of boot camp usually go on to attain great things while serving in The Corps. The more "motivated and squared away" they are, the more achievement, commendations, rank, and status amongst fellow Marines are rewarded and granted.

The majority of Devil Dogs love that life. They live that life. The USMC enhances that mind-set by encouraging each individual to give it all they've got. Sitting in a fighting hole drenched in mud and rain isn't that bad when you're sharing home life with your buddy. When you're on a twenty-mile hike ordered by your company commander, because it's about troop readiness or because it's Friday, completely sucks until you reach the finish line with your squad members together. Each one of us was loaded down with body armor, an eighty-pound rucksack, and a weapon till our toes were numbed out and cold, hungry for a real meal other than dried crackers with peanut butter and dehydrated pork chow mein. The best possible way to take our minds off all of that was a mixture of dark humor and platoon cohesion, AKA camaraderie in civilian terms.

The downtime for most first-time enlisted Marines is equally aggressive. With similarities to a college student between eighteen and twenty-two, who is away from home for the first time, an estimated 60 to 80 percent of service members party till absolute obliteration. How many cases of beer and shots of whiskey or tequila a Marine can consume in one night is a bragging right the next day. Chasing tail on the off time, AKA liberty, was the main objective for the evening. On many deployments, Marines and Sailors go to places like Hong Kong, Singapore, Phuket, Mombasa, UAE, Kuwait, Iraq, Australia, and Hawaii. With all of that culture from various places around the world, they can honestly tell you more about the bar scenes and social lifestyles than about the museums or tourist attractions. Good or bad, it was one of the most memorable moments of their lives even if they didn't realize it. They worked hard and partied even harder. If you couldn't carry your own weight or needed help, then you were a "shitbag" and usually met with a lot of static from other Marines.

The Washout Factor

For a lot of people who join the military, the experience is not a good a time for them. Some barely squeak by in boot camp, and that level of Marine is very noticeable compared to the men and women who are "motivated and squared away." They constantly struggle with basic issues like uniforms, PT, proper body weight, and/or severe personal discipline issues. Think of the character Gomer Pyle in the movie *Full Metal Jacket*. The type of Marine depicted in that film is actually pretty accurate. They always seem to cause problems for their platoon and are usually frowned upon as the oddball of the group. In the Marine world, they are known as the "shit bag."

For the most part, Marines of that caliber usually wash out, and it may happen immediately or over a length of time. Invariably they hit a point where they can go no further in service, and it is unfortunate. When a washout happens, benefits are lost, pride has taken one hell of a blow, and there can be a heavy feeling of failure as they are sent home.

For other service members, another unfortunate situation can occur. Sometimes an individual may end up in a regiment or battalion that has been plagued with problems and/or poor leadership. The Armed Forces work hard to minimize such situations, but it does happen. Other times, recruits can wind up with a certain group of men and women or under a command with whom they just do not mix well. There is an unfortunate divide between that individual and his or her unit that can cause resentments and quarrels that may consume the person entirely. It is not something that individual had expected when he or she enlisted. It is just an unfortunate chain of events that can cause a very bad set of circumstances for that particular individual.

If you were one of those Marines or service members who felt that way or went through that kind of experience, the descriptions I am using here are in reference to how the military might have felt like to you, but that is not who you were/are. It was just a bad time for you, and many service members who were motivated and/or squared away, a lot of times, struggled with the same difficulties you did when they get home. Each one of you had certain issues that prevented you from performing your duties, and in many cases, you were judged harshly. Do not view this as anything other than general observations.

THE
TRANSITION

AFTER THE FIRST ENLISTMENT term is up for Marines, they have the option to either reenlist or get out with an honorable discharge. Right now, the reenlistments are as low as one in five, and those who do stay in serve longer terms or become "lifer Marines" and serve their full twenty years. For the most part, lifers usually tone down the partying with age, maturity, and rank progression.

However, things are quite different for first termers. The standard enlistment package for any service Marine is four years. And for four years (or more if there was a reenlistment), that individual moved with a purpose and got the job done as fast as humanly possible, no matter what it took or what the personal cost. And everything that person knows how to do is exactly that way. Most Marines who are almost done with their service contract, AKA short-timers, are usually crossing the days off the calendar till they go home. They start blowing off formations and inspections just because they know they can get away with it. They are full of excitement looking forward to getting back to their old civilian life and their families.

It was called Temp for Taps when I was getting out in 2001, but according to a Marine brother of mine who is just now getting out, it is now called TRP, or Transitional Readiness Program. It is a seven-day course given to all Marines who are in the final weeks of their service contract. It includes résumé building, interviewing skills, job searches, and VA resources, and a small portion is given for what to expect once the Marine gets home.

As the discharge date gets closer, the thought of military life being over sounds pretty good to most service members. He or she can go home for good! The soon to be a veteran can hang out with old friends and family that have been missed since joining the military. No more formations. No more inspections. No more PT at 0530. There is a sense of true freedom and liberty as the obligations set forth in the enlistment contract have all been met. There are benefits waiting as soon as they cross the finish line. There is a great feeling of pride and accomplishment in most service members given they had followed through on everything that was in front of them. Even if there were parts of the job and activities they hated or did not like to do, none of that matters anymore. It's over, no more—FREEDOM!

For most Marines, there is probably a little savings in the bank (if anything at all) and an idea of where they will go look for work or what school they want to attend. Parties are thrown by fellow Marines, a plane ticket is used, and in a few short hours the "life" as a Marine is *over*.

The Honeymoon Phase

Upon release from service, everyone for the most part is happy his or her loved one is finally home for good, and more parties are thrown in the veteran's honor. People want to hear about the experience, and many "thank you for your service" and pats on the back are given. It typically is a very euphoric time, and most veterans may feel like a rock star and enjoy taking the time off to unwind. This period can last anywhere from a month or up to

two years in most cases; however, times and situations vary for different veterans.

As days turn to weeks and months turn to years, friends and family start to notice the changes and differences in the veteran. In most cases, unless there is a family member or close friend who has been in the veteran's shoes, people around the veteran do not like the changes they are seeing. The honeymoon phase begins to end simply due to the fact that the veteran is never going back to service. The adjustment starts to become a very real challenge for the veteran.

The Isolation Begins

The way he or she eats. The way the veteran speaks. Carries himself or herself. Drinks too much. Cusses too much. Moves too fast. Is too aggressive. Is too loud. Can be a bully. Needs to slow down. Appears irritable. Can't sit still. Wakes up at odd hours. Impulsive behavior. Reckless activity. These are just a few things that may manifest themselves quickly or over an extended period of time. It starts to concern people close to the veteran, and they start to worry or resent the veteran as time progresses.

The veteran reacts by giving an "I don't need you" attitude toward friends and family, and as the resentment builds, the accomplishments inside tells the veteran that he or she can deal with any situation. "I can handle this" is the attitude engrained in the veteran. This deception is built on an internal foundation that carried him or her through service and actually made them a great Marine or soldier. However, the saying "once a Marine always a Marine" is in direct contrast to the real-life situation he or she is in. The veteran does not realize that being a Marine in a civilian world does *not* work.

As arguments and disagreements surface, people in the heat of emotion tell the veteran, "You're not a Marine anymore!" That is where the two worlds collide and become very confusing for the veteran. Unfortunately, the veteran does not realize that he or she is sinking into a dangerous place.

The Missing Chain of Command

For many service members, especially first-termers, the presence of authority figures—that is, officers and/or senior NCOs—were an essential part of getting the best out of that particular individual. There was always someone there to tell him or her when and how to get things done, and without that authority there, service members sometimes enjoyed the opportunity to *skate* (to slack off or blow off your duties). For the most part, trained officers and good leadership can figure ways to dial in that individual Marine and do it in a way where the individual responds with respect and good proficiency. Of course, in order to pass boot camp, following orders had now become a permanent fixture as part of his or her job. It takes some getting used to for some Marines, and for others, it comes very easily.

When the veteran goes home permanently, that authority is now obsolete--permanently. The veteran has to find the discipline from within in order to maintain forward progress with his or her daily life. Unfortunately, with that authority no longer there, the discipline can fade rather quickly for many veterans. The enticement to want to just sleep and party all day can be too much for some individuals; therefore, the problems begin to mount rather quickly.

Author's Note: This may seem like a perfect match in explaining many veterans' behaviors. However, another point is very important and must be understood. Any veteran who received an honorable discharge or left the military in good standings had to endure a number of years of a completely different kind of discipline compared to civilian discipline.

There is a view of the general public that service members endure yelling and screaming of orders throughout their entire contract. This line of thinking is a fallacy. The yelling and screaming of orders lasts for about a year or so or until the service member has learned the ins and outs of his or her particular branch of service and duties. After that, however, the service member's daily progression morphs from being *told* what to do to what he or she is *expected* to do. As long as the service member adheres to the guidelines and direction of superiors, he or she is usually treated with calm, professionalism, and respect, and the service member moves up in rank with relative ease. Of course, if he or she steps out of line or disobeys orders, then it can be an entirely different scenario of pure hell.

THE
DIFFERENCES

An Unexpected Confusion

DISORIENTATION WOULD FALL ON any individual in the civilian world who makes any one or more of the following major changes in their life: a career change, relocation of where he or she lives, new friends, and/or a new lifestyle. For the civilian, in most cases, these changes are understood and met with a lot of compassion from his or her supervisors, fellow colleagues, family, and friends.

However, things can be quite different for veterans.

This form of disorientation is on steroids subconsciously in the mind of a veteran due to the fact that he or she just made *all* of these changes without even realizing it by coming home. Even though most associations of the veteran are with friends and family from before enlistment, they were not the main focal point of the veteran's life during those years while in service. There's a lot about their veteran that is completely unknown and new to them, and all they remember was the young man or woman who got on a plane years ago for boot camp. Yes, the veteran may have come home often to visit, but those visits rarely lasted more than a couple of weeks.

Before long, life can start to get a little challenging for the individual. The veteran, who is the new guy or girl in the workforce, back amongst family and friends, and back home for good, is now starting to accumulate behaviors that are odd and off-putting to a lot of people around him or her. "There is something not right with him or her" is murmured among family members and friends. In many instances, the understanding between civilians can be easier to understand amongst other civilians, and the veteran can pick up on that. It can easily make the veteran feel as if he or she is an oddball and is being mistreated and/or targeted. Therefore, the divide between veterans and civilians begins to reach a noticeable difference.

BEHAVIORAL DIFFERENCES

The Eating

In boot camp, recruits are given five to ten minutes to eat an entire tray of food, depending on their branch of service. In the field, it's MREs and COMRATS. When the Marine does end up back in garrison or on liberty, the taste alone of good food turns the

Marine's mouth into a vacuum cleaner. PT, training, and the number of calories being consumed every day create an insatiable appetite.

After the Marine's first year or so of boot training and constant on the go, eating like that becomes second nature, and it is then carried for the next three years or more all the way till when the Marine goes home. It's not weird. It's not that he or

she needs to slow down. It's not stress. It's not that he or she is in a hurry. It's just how the veteran eats now. Period.

Civilians who are at the table with the veteran can feel inclined tell him or her, "Slow down and enjoy your meal." That shit gets really old after a while. You never hear a veteran tell a civilian, "Hey, fat ass, pick up the pace. We got things to do today." A bit of advice to civilians: let the veteran eat in peace.

The Tone and Speech

A Marine is given a simple job by his or her superiors:

> *Example 1*
>
> Empty this storage area, organize it, and make room for new gear coming in. The senior Marine—usually a junior NCO or NCO—is given a small work crew of three Marines to help, but ultimately the job falls on the senior Marine, who begins to delegate and figure how he or she wants to get the job done. The instructions are explained as follows:
>
> **(Warning: Explicit language alert!)**
>
> Senior Marine says, "Smith, take that crap out of the storage and set it over here. Rodriguez, unfuck all these boxes and make them look good. The rest of us are going to get into that shitbox and unfuck that mess. Good to go? Good! Let's go."
>
> Smith starts pulling boxes and staging them in the wrong place.
>
> Senior Marine says, "Goddamn it, Smith! You are dumber than a bag of hammers! I said *over there!*"

All of the Marines, including Smith, take the insults rather lightly and may even laugh it off and carry on.

Rodriguez stops for a second to get a drink of water, and senior Marine says, "Hey, fuck-stick Rodriguez! I know you beaners are naturally slow, but get off your ass and let's wrap this up." Once again, a massive round of laughter comes from everyone due to the fact that they know each other and that rearranging a storage box is actually very light work, therefore, they have fun with it.

The only time there is no laughter is when the job is under a time constraint or if the crew is not or has not gotten along. All orders and dialect coming from senior Marine are sharp and stern usually accompanied with moderate to aggressive volume. The junior Marines laugh with it and take it lightly because they know that none of it is meant to be taken personally and they are junior to the senior. One day they will be the senior.

For the most part, this is how work is done inside the USMC. The level of intensity and unique humor differs between units and platoons based on many variables that include but are not limited to the following: the individual Marine, unity and understanding between the Marines, whether the work crew is motivated or a shit-bag crew, dynamics, and the type of leadership being demonstrated—fear leader or respect leader. However, the amplitude and level of intensity are usually this high.

In the civilian world, almost all of this method of work would be considered offensive, vulgar, bullying, unprofessional, mean, and, in some cases, grounds for dismissal. It worked for the veteran while on active duty, and he or she does not understand why his or her civilian coworkers are not responding the same way. While on active duty, that particular way of doing things was usually praised and made sense, yet the same task in the civilian world, with civilian workers, is a total bust. The tension grows and creates conflict at work that can cause the veteran's unhappiness with his or her job, poor cohesion with supervisors and fellow employees, termination, and/or the need to "find something else."

Example 2

Another issue with speech and tone goes back to amplitude. Forward progress in any branch of military is achieved in the form of seniority and rank, and in order to do so, veterans were taught how to lead by service members that were senior to them. Assertiveness, confidence, and ability to give clear and concise orders in a military manner enable the service member to take on more responsibilities and a higher billet of duties.

Take that mentality into an employee meeting or a group discussion over a company issue in the civilian world, and it is not a good mix. When given an opportunity to speak at said meeting, the veteran will stand and state his or her opinion with much of that seasoned assertiveness, confidence, and planning in a military fashion. The veteran's tone is clear and sharp, and opinions and/or ideas are stated in a very direct manner. To civilians, it comes across as a bull in a china shop or crude and aggressive. Fellow employees and supervisors may feel inclined to inform the veteran, with the best of intentions and not to offend, that he or she needs to "tone it down. Don't be so passionate." In a lot of these instances, the veteran has no clue what he or she said or did that needs to be "toned down."

After repeated moments like these, confusion and doubt can grow in the mind of the veteran, and begins to question his or her own actions. "Maybe I am a bully" or "Perhaps I am too aggressive" enters the thought process and is in total conflict with everything that had been developed and taught while in service. "Things are not making any sense anymore" is what takes hold and pre-occupies the mind of the veteran.

The Dark Humor
Let these examples speak for themselves. **(Be advised. The language utilized in this section is very graphic.)**

Example 1

Two Marines have just dug a fighting hole for a training op, and they decide to take a minute to have noon chow. As they open their MREs, Marine A has jalapeno/cheese, and Marine B has peanut butter.

Marine B says to Marine A, "What do you want to trade for your jalapeno/cheese?"

Marine A replies, "Let me slide my penis into your sister's ass."

Marine B responds, "Deal."

Example 2

Marine A is working under a truck and can't reach a tool laying nearby.

Marine A says to Marine B, "Hand me that wrench."

Marine B replies, "You wanna put your hand on my tool. What?"

Marine A says again with a little more aggression, "Dude, the wrench."

Marine B responds again, "I don't roll that way. Maybe Herrera will let you feel his tool. But not me."

Marine A, jokingly pissed, then says, "Goddamn it, Smitty! Gimme the fucking wrench!"

Marine B hands Marine A the wrench and replies at the same time, "Here you go, motherfucker. Next time you wanna grab my tool, I'm gonna charge your ass some fuckin' money!"

They all laugh, and this exchange will go on and on for hours.

Example 3

Two Marines who are roommates are getting ready to head into town for liberty. One is white, and the other is Hispanic. They've been in field all week, and a hot pizza, cold beer, and women are all they want. One is ready; the other is still getting dressed.

"Hey, you fuckin' spick! Move your ass!" says the white Marine.

The Hispanic replies, "Whatever, you fuckin' cracker! Your mom never complained this much when I used to take her out, *puto!*"

The humor demonstrated here is nowhere near as vulgar as it can get, yet none of it is taken personally amongst them. Something about Marines working, training, PT-ing, and bonding as a platoon allows for an absolute truthful understanding whom each Marine is to the other. Racism is virtually nonexistent. (It's still there, just not as sensitive as civilian life.) There are times when a line can be crossed, and fists are thrown. However, they are very rare. When the humor does get to a point of a fight, punches are thrown, and usually after that, handshakes are given to each other, the disagreement is brushed off, and the fire is put out.

Any civilian on the receiving of that kind of sass or humor is highly likely to take offense, say some form of retort or resentment, and where it escalates from there varies. Take that same humor, tone it way down by hundredfold, and clean it up, and it would still be too offensive around even the closest circles of civilian friends and family of the veteran. Awkward silences become frequent as a result, and dirty looks are given to the veteran as if pure filth were all they heard.

Personal beefs can lead to assault charges, and because the service member has been military trained, he or she is the one to be ostracized or charged more harshly. Technically, dark humor really is pretty vulgar stuff, just not to the veteran.

The Irritable and Restless Behavior

With these few illustrations of military lifestyle, one can conclude that military behavior is highly inappropriate in a civilian setting. Therefore, as more and more differences come to light over time, the divide grows between civilians and the veteran. Due to constant bombardment of bad days with little incidents and comments about how weird, vulgar, and/or crude the veteran is, frustration in the veteran can grow exponentially, both consciously and subconsciously.

In many cases, civilians do try their best to give veterans all they can to help, and they are genuinely concerned about that individual veteran's well-being. What can be irritating and completely baffling is why the veteran is not responding with positive results. It is neither the civilian's nor the veteran's fault. It can be as simple as the mental lens the civilian and veteran are looking through that causes a lot of miscommunication and misunderstanding. The civilian cannot see or understand what the veteran sees and vice versa.

MENTAL DIFFERENCES

Finances

There is a significant contrast between military and civilian discipline that can perhaps have one of the biggest impacts on transition for veterans. The general public, in many instances, is drawn to the idea of good discipline for young adults, or lack thereof, to encourage their son or daughter to enlist or pursue a life in the military. However, there is a big difference to the meaning of the word *"discipline"* between civilians and the Armed Forces.

Military discipline is geared more toward controlling fear, assertiveness, confidence, bearing, self- sacrifice, good teamwork, following instructions, mastering various combat tactics, body control, and learning how to demonstrate what they've been taught under high-stress conditions. Above all, service members use these disciplines to perform all of their duties while keeping the upmost professionalism of the United States Armed forces. While these disciplines are critical to developing a well-rounded, strong military service member, they are not really needed as much in the civilian world.

Civilian discipline is centered more around obtaining and maintaining a steady job or gainful employment which in turn enables individual independence and stability. Eventually things move forward to further disciplines like finding or building a good home, making car payments, obtaining adequate living capitol to afford decent grocery shopping and other household amenities, paying the bills and taxes, and providing for themselves and their families.

In other words, *finances.*

Finances are the bedrock of civilian stability to include the basics such as savings, a solid budgeting plan, emergency money, and future securities and investments. Service members are largely grossly uneducated as to how important this truly is during their first enlistments, therefore causing an incredible amount of problems for a lot of them when they get out.

Let's go deeper on this issue.

Most young adults between the ages of eighteen to twenty-four begin to develop and refine habits that will carry them for the rest of their lives, and how they spend money, for better or worse, can play a big role in that. Service members on their first enlistment are, for the most part, housed inside barracks and fed at the chow hall. Therefore, there is little to no need to develop the civilian basics, that is, rent, utilities, and groceries. While this is an absolute essential need to develop new service members into qualified professional Marines and Soldiers, the lack of need for managing basic living expenses at this age may actually handicap a lot of service members down the road. The temptation to spend their paychecks frivolously is quite an enticement given they know they still have a roof over their heads and hot breakfast in the morning.

Young adults in the civilian world have to face financial responsibility in a different way if they want to obtain their own independence and stability and move out of their parents' house.

These two separate directions of young adult development can perhaps explain why one of the biggest struggles that veterans face in the civilian world are finances and good spending habits, which, when mismanaged, can lead to homelessness. With that said, perhaps financial responsibility should be further examined and emphasized within first-term military service members.

Let's go even deeper on this issue.

There is a stigma in the civilian world, unfortunately, that you are a loser if you don't have any money and can't even afford your own needs. We as an American culture tend to look at stability and personal worth based on how much money you have, and this can play a big part in causing conflict for the veteran at home. All the civilian can see is a veteran constantly asking for money over and over and may even make hasty remarks like, "You need to be more responsible." This, in turn, can enrage the veteran very easily.

While one young adult in the civilian world was learning what it costs to take care of himself or herself and their family in a *financial capacity*, the other who was in the military was learning what it costs to take care of himself or herself and their country in a *fighting capacity*. The veterans had to mentally discipline themselves, be prepared to sacrifice themselves, and overcome their own fears, an immense challenge that civilians do not have to experience.

Simply stated, the two different cultures, civilian compared to military, take two separate paths of developing young adult discipline. As the service member is discharged and thrown back into the sea of civilian life, he or she can be completely ill prepared to handle civilian financial responsibility, thereby increasing the level of adjustment struggles.

There Is No Such Thing as Failure

"Failure is not an option." Perhaps you have heard that expression, and in a military setting, that mentality is an absolute necessity. However, if you reflect on that concept, one could surmise that it is mostly a form of mental conditioning. In the military—and much more intense in the Infantry—failure equals death, and/or failure of a mission can lead to death. That is where amplitude, integrity, military discipline, and fortitude that were ingrained from the very beginning serve the best purpose. Good Marines learn that art, and great Marines become experts at exploiting that philosophy in everything they do. The military, and especially the Marine Corps, when engaged in combat and throughout their training, does not compromise their principles, position, objective, mission, and each other ... *ever.*

In the civilian world, failure is a part of everyday life and it is everywhere. Businesses, partnerships, financial endeavors, projects, career pursuits, marriages, and personal relationships are all examples of civilian journeys (*missions* in military terms) that can fail or succeed. The big and obvious difference is that these are not life-and-death situations for the most part.

Accepting failure is a natural part of civilian life due to the fact that most civilian competition—be it personal, recreational, or business—has room for only one first place. If civilians cannot achieve that first place, that can be labeled and/or felt as failure and even more so to a veteran. That is where the term *failure* can take on a different approach and is called *compromise* or *learning experiences.* And it's in everything.

Compromise is the cornerstone of allowing a civil society to move forward, and a Marine or service member is not used to that on most levels. Many aspects of daily life in the civilian world demand compromise, both consciously and subconsciously. Personal relationships, work-related business, and daily interactions with civilian surroundings all call for a time to acknowledge the other party's point of view and be willing to accept a happy medium.

Granted, as a society, we are struggling with compromises on all levels. However, even more so for a veteran, they can be very disorienting and feel very odd and/or out of place. Veterans were trained over and over not to compromise themselves, the mission, adherence to direction, and/or position. If they had any doubts or did not want to follow the orders given or the line of thought, there was no option. The orders are followed, or the Marine or service member would find himself or herself in very deep trouble. Disobedience is absolutely not tolerated at all.

Get the Job Done

Another form of adjustment conflict for veterans may come in the different methods of civilian pace of daily business. Veterans were trained to move from point A to point B in the quickest and most efficient way possible. "Get the job done and put some fire in it while you're doing it!!"

Civilians move quite differently.

First, there has to be an email sent out. Then there has to be a discussion or a meeting to contemplate the issue. Then there's a few weeks of trading phone calls and emails before a second meeting is called. Then there has to be a plan put in place that is developed over time, and in most cases, if it is not financially viable or too risky, then the issue is dismissed rather quickly. Based on this illustration, it can be concluded that the civilian world does not move from point A to point B. It moves from point A to point A.1. Then to A.2. Then to A.3 subclause 1 and so on.

This may be an exaggeration, but issues like cost are usually not a problem in the military. There are usually sufficient resources, personnel, and equipment to get anything done, and speed and intensity are usually an absolute priority.

Being at Ease with the Differences

Every one of these mental and behavioral differences between military and civilian cultures require some serious personal adjustment from veterans on multiple levels if they want to have a successful and peaceful, easy going civilian life. Veterans can become frustrated with the different ways of doing business and struggle to get accustomed to civilian line of thinking. They have to learn and refine civilian etiquette if they want to fit in with their colleagues or peers. They have to adjust their business manner and work ethics to civilian methods and pace if they want to obtain and maintain solid employment. They have to closely monitor their financial changes between military and civilian pay checks and spending or else their budget can spiral out of control very easily. They have to learn to be at peace with bad investments, failures, and compromising themselves and their position. And lastly, they must allow other opinions from their peers around them if they are to achieve conformity to society.

A Personal Note

Right this very second, as I'm writing this, there is an active service member who I just shared a smoke with who is about to be discharged from the Navy due to health issues. He's a great guy with a good heart and a true love for what he does. He's the kind of guy who would give you the shirt off his back if he thought you needed it more. It's all gone for him in the next couple of weeks or so. Today he's been drinking hard liquor very heavily since last night, and he's still going. He has consumed a gallon of vodka and intermixing other various liquors, and he is only on his second day of the binge.

I cornered him and hit him with it. "Say, man. You're in a really bad spot right now. You're depressed as hell and masking it with all this party. You've got a bad case of the fuck-its right now, don't you?"

His response was, "Yeah, man. I know. I'm fucked up. I can't sleep, but let's talk about you." (This was clearly clinical deflection.)

This is really hard to for me watch simply because I know how high the odds are for what's next for this guy. I've been in his shoes, and I know thousands more just like him who are totally stuck. Unfortunately, a miracle needs to happen, and he's on the verge of becoming another statistic. God be with him.

ISOLATION TAKES ROOT

ḀS TIME PROGRESSES, SOMETIMES months or years after their EAS, the differences and resentments begin to feel very burdensome. The veteran may find that he or she is struggling in all aspects of living. Job problems are wearing out finances, and friends are "getting tired of his or her shit." Problems paying bills and keeping a healthy home with a significant other can become an everyday challenge. Unfortunately, the significant other can usually wind up becoming the target for the release of all that anger and frustration, therefore opening the door for domestic abuse. With all of this disarray in the veteran's life, it can be very hard to see how the hell life became so difficult.

Impulsive to Just Plain Crazy
The pent-up energy that used to be channeled through the veteran's job while in service, mixed in with frustration and disorientation, can produce massive amounts of anxiety and discomfort for the veteran, thereby causing him or her to seek release or refuge. Sleeping and eating habits begin to change for the worse. Alienation from close family and pulling disappearing acts become more frequent. Impulsive and radical behavior can grow and somehow seem to make more sense to the veteran rather than to keep enduring this ridiculous amount of difference between the veteran and society. Sooner or later, the veteran begins to explore stronger methods of release that can do far more harm than good.

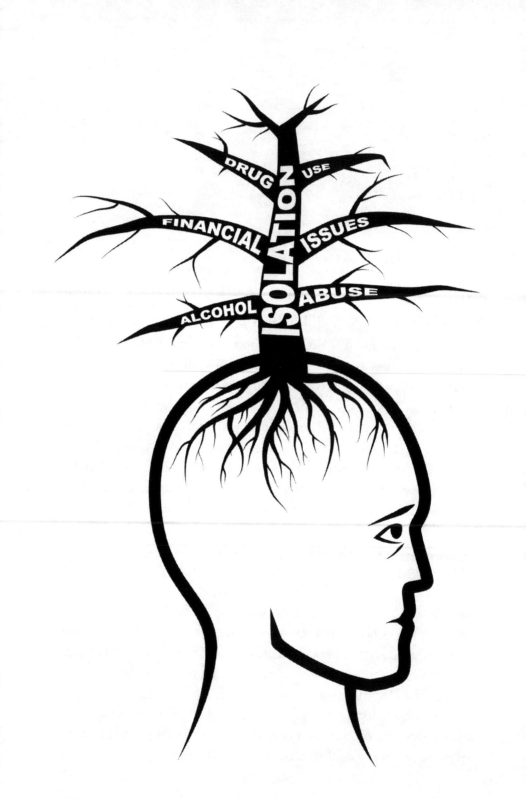

Drugs and Alcohol

For many veterans, an alcohol or substance abuse problem may have already begun while in service without even knowing it. As explained earlier, a hard party lifestyle is very common while in service, and after the honeymoon phase draws to an end, the veteran is confronted with his or her own internal discipline to decide whether to tone down the party life or keep going. The veteran may have already passed the threshold of the ability to control it on their own; therefore, drinking heavily and hard partying may have already become a natural part of life.

For those veterans who do tone it down, they are still confronted with the challenges of adjustment, as are the veterans who are already sick with alcoholism or substance abuse. Either way, with all of the complications and adjustment problems going through the veteran's mind, the parties and bar scenes become a place of refuge and release.

What had begun as a recreational party favor has now become an essential part of life to get the veteran through the day.

A Bad Case of the Fuck-Its

Eventually the veteran snaps and both literally and internally says, "Fuck it!" It is a form of complete subconscious and cognitive shutdown. Secluding himself or herself from everybody and everything is the easiest way to make all the mess go away. Mind-altering substances morph into a drug or alcohol problem that lead to hard-core erratic behavior—theft, prostitution, heavy and more graphic pornography, drug binges, and/or obscene amounts of alcohol consumption. Finances and credit have become a mess. The veteran's other half has had enough and wants out of the relationship, and if kids are involved, they're gone too.

In a lot of cases, recklessness can lead to breaking the law; therefore, criminal records begin to grow, and the patience of the justice system starts to wear thin. Reckless and impulsive behavior has now changed to completely radical and extreme. A lot of times, veterans will realize the worry and concern from their loved ones and would rather disappear, thinking it would be better off for everyone.

Even worse, the veteran flat-out doesn't give a shit anymore about anybody or anything.

Becoming a Statistic

Now we are heading to the unfortunate tragic part, for both the veteran and his or her family, where former military personnel become an awful civilian statistic. Theft, drug-related crimes, alcoholism, addiction, broken homes, homelessness, domestic abuse, assault, murder, and, the worst of the worst, suicide all take place on or around this phase.

People, both veterans and civilians, need to stop and think for a minute. The veteran in that state of circumstances, for the majority, did not get off the plane homeless, totally crazy, or even suicidal. (This does not apply to PTSD veterans.) A sad, tragic turn of events had to have taken place to get the veteran to that point of complete mental breakdown.

Rock bottom is what it's called. The well is empty. There is nothing left inside in any capacity—finances, job, family, or good memories. It's all gone. This bottom usually comes in the form of an arrest, hard desperation, a car accident or something similar, and/or completely strung out on booze or drugs. The once energetic, positively motivated spirit inside the veteran is completely broken in half. The amount of confusion and depression is completely overbearing, and the veteran looks in the mirror and can see nothing more than an absolute disgrace.

For a lot of veterans, family and friends can turn on them, and the veteran becomes the butt of some ignorant jokes or is completely cast out. The veteran is ostracized sometimes intentionally and other times not. Holiday gatherings and social functions can become very awkward with someone like that around; therefore, people start avoiding the veteran all together. A threshold has been reached within family and friends and they are at a complete loss of what to do to help the veteran. "I was gonna call you, but I just got too busy" or "That weirdo can't handle himself or herself anymore and is out of control." Sadly, this can be the stopping point for a lot of veterans.

Suicide is the chosen path.

A CRY FOR HELP

FOR THOSE WHO DO manage to gather together enough willpower to move on, they mostly reach out to other veterans, family, and/or mental health professionals. Unfortunately, in most cases, life has to get to the point of desperate times in order for the veteran to reach out for help. Along with that, there usually is a certain feeling of embarrassment that comes with the understanding of the need for help; therefore, only trusted sources are the first ones who are reluctantly turned to. Even worse, that state of mind is accompanied with many other issues as mentioned before, like addiction, financial desperation, possible prison sentences, inability to sustain gainful employment, a broken family, and/or suicidal tendencies. It is fair to say there is an "elephant in the room" that follows the veteran everywhere he or she goes. That's putting it lightly. It's more like a herd of elephants with a gorilla beating down on his or her back. With so many desperate circumstances, it can be very difficult for the individual to identify the root of the problem. On top of that, the time and willpower alone that it takes to actually get in to see a professional requires a deep personal commitment from within the veteran if there is to be any solid chance at recovery.

Alcoholism and substance abuse, in a lot of cases, are the bigger issues. The veteran's recklessness and impulsivity has now morphed into a long list of bad habits that can be defined as self-destructive behavior. When recovery is attempted, the larger underlying issues causing problems must be first addressed before the real healing can begin.

Relapse, unfortunately, is a given part of the recovery process. Digressing back to drugs, alcohol, promiscuous sexual activity, reckless spending, late night parties and all forms of self-destructive behavior are very easy to happen for each individual. This, in turn, causes the process to have to start all over again and the revolving door at rehabilitation facilities can easily become the next cycle of the veteran's life.

Recovery Breakdown

In a lot of ways, the healing part for the veteran is the next phase and is an entirely different world of its own. When the time comes where he or she finally admits that there is a problem (done with denying the problem), recovery is the solution that is needed to get things back on track. This can be a very confusing, dark time for both the veteran and his or her family members. There are literally hundreds of various different methods of professional treatment, along with personal opinions and resources from loved ones. Family and friends do their best to interject on what they've heard or feel they know about people struggling with mental issues, and a lot of times, the veteran can feel like he or she has little say on what to do for treatment.

One thing must be understood from the very beginning. Recovery is neither an overnight process nor a one-time experience for most people. Quitting bad habits "cold turkey" (stopping all the self-destructive habits on their own recognizance) can happen, but those cases are very rare. In truth, recovery is a long, drawn-out process that involves a lot of patience, perseverance, commitment, and humility for all parties involved.

Minimizing the Problem

With so many advances in the fields of technology and medical attention, we as a society have become accustomed to having our problems resolved instantaneously. If you have a headache, you take an aspirin or ibuprofen. If you break an arm or a leg, you go the hospital and get a cast. Other ailments such as cancer or diabetes have clear medical identifiers such as a tumor or poor blood sugar levels. Hence there is no denying that there is a problem with that individual, along with a lot of sympathy and compassion from loved ones. Unfortunately, it is not that easy in the world of mental illness. It is a cloudy, grey world in which a lot of time and change are required for each individual in order to resolve the problem. Therapists and the veteran have to unravel the issues of the past piece by piece in order to keep them from coming back (relapse). After the issues are identified, the veteran must be willing to accept the changes that are necessary in his or her life in order for recovery to be successful and furthermore, make those necessary changes a reality.

For many veterans, as explained earlier, the confusion and disarray in their life can create a level of deception for themselves and their families. It took a moment of desperation for the veteran to reach out, and once the hopelessness has calmed, he or she can immediately begin to feel better. (Individual results vary.) Once a small amount of confidence returns, it can deceive the veteran into thinking he or she can handle it on their own from there. The veteran's own mind can play tricks and it may feel as if he or she no longer needs professional help nor anymore recovery support.

Family members and close loved ones, in some cases, unintentionally can also be an obstacle to gainful recovery. Everyone, including the veteran, just wants things to go back to the way they were in the quickest, smoothest, quietest possible manner. Embarrassment can be too overwhelming for both the veteran and his or her family; therefore, the essential requirements needed to achieve gainful recovery might be taken with many shortcuts. However, recovery and mental rehabilitation are not a light switch that can be turned off, and for the most part, the veteran may have to change a great deal about himself or herself in order to get a serious grip on recovery.

Professional Help

When a veteran takes a seat in front of a counselor, social worker, and/or professional therapist for the first time, they begin to break down the issues together that are the biggest problems in the veteran's life. The average length of any therapeutic session is about an hour or so; therefore, in that small period of time, a knot of problems the size of a spaghetti bowl is laid out in front of the therapist to assess and define what is going on with the veteran. It is highly impossible to gain a clear understanding of the root problems within that length of time; therefore, follow-up appointments are essential. Much like fingerprints, each individual veteran has accumulated a unique set of problems, bad habits, and self-destructive behaviors that prevent the individual from moving forward with his or her life.

For a veteran, many times, given he or she may have had better days while in uniform, it can be easily diagnosed or categorized that he or she is possibly suffering from PTSD and/or other mental illnesses like bi-polar disorder or substance abuse. Treatment plans are then put into action to begin recovery for the veteran, and depending on whichever diagnosis is given by the veteran's therapists, rehabilitation programs are dialed in to match certain criteria for his or her specific needs.

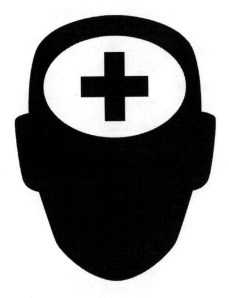

MENTAL HEALTH THERAPY

THE DIAGNOSTICS AND STATISTICAL Manual (DSM-5) along with other professional mental health resources are common tools used by therapists and social workers to help identify the underlying issues that plague each individual veteran. As explained earlier in the text, the veteran and professional therapist discuss in great lengths all the possible variables that can be contributors to the veteran's despair.

As of this moment, the following forms of diagnosis and therapy tracks are the most widely referred to for treatment for veterans struggling with mental health issues. Treatment regimens vary for each individual; however, these examples are based on eleven years of firsthand experiences and observations. All definitions are paraphrased from the National Institute of Mental Health (NIMH) and DSM-5 and are in layman's terms.

Post-Traumatic Stress Disorder (PTSD)

Post-Traumatic Stress Disorder, or PTSD, is a psychiatric disorder that can occur following the experience or witnessing of a life-threatening event such as military combat, natural disasters, terrorist incidents, serious accidents, or physical or sexual assault in adult or childhood.

Symptoms of PTSD are to include but not limited to the following: irritable or aggressive behavior; anxiousness or inability to sit still; anxiety; problems with concentration; lack of focus; erratic behavior; isolation; depression; culture shock; anger; mood swings; sleep irregularities; improper diet; and/or self-destructive behaviors.

Anxiety Disorder

Anxiety disorder can be characterized as a group of mental issues that cause massive amounts of stress, fear, and/or worry within the body. Some medical facts have concluded that obscene amounts of cortisol in the stomach or the body's internal habit of releasing too much adrenaline, especially when it is not needed, can be key factors in producing massive amounts of anxiety. In other instances, too much caffeine, substance abuse and/or nicotine can also be the culprit. There are several different kinds of anxiety disorders but for the most part they generally can create unbearable feelings of fear, worry, restlessness, insomnia, irritability, and sometimes a strong feeling of impending doom.

Bi-Polar

Bi-Polar can also be known as the swing between the body's two internal poles and has different levels of severity. When on the high side, there can be strong feelings of assertiveness, energy, and impulsivity. Bi-Polar, in this state, can create problems for the individual by resulting in reckless or impulsive behaviors. There is also a strong drive to get everything done all at once and can disrupt healthy sleep habits by creating temporary insomnia.

When the pole swings to the opposite direction, the individual may feel overly depressed. He or she may have lack of confidence, low energy levels, and/or the feeling of burnout. This, in turn, can result in the inability to get out of bed or get up and face the day's normal challenges. Poles can change at random or perhaps with no set pattern; hence maintaining long-term daily progression in employment and/or social interactions can become a challenge.

Intermittent Explosive Disorder, AKA Rageaholic

Rageaholic can be defined as a person who can get a high or a rush the more enraged he or she is. This person can also be prone to massive fits of anger and rage with little to no thought or provocation.

Social Phobia

Social phobia is the fear of being around and/or involved in social situations or settings. Public restaurants, crowded movie theaters, and/or shopping malls are examples of places the individual will avoid, no matter the cost. Isolation from family, loved ones, friends, and people in general allows the person to feel better rather than to deal with said fear. This can also lead to a form of social anxiety, which can create unwanted nervousness or discomfort for the individual, especially around crowded environments.

Clinical Depression

Clinical depression can be defined as a more intense version of depression disorder, which can lead to feelings of never-ending sadness and/or hopelessness.

It sometimes can be attributed to a thyroid issue. Insomnia, poor eating habits, isolation, massive amounts of sleep without the feeling of rest, and severe mood swings can all be attributed to Clinical Depression.

Attention Deficit Hyperactive Disorder (ADHD)
Attention Deficit Hyperactive Disorder (ADHD) is most commonly diagnosed in children; however, there are many cases of individuals who can carry this disorder into adulthood. Its characteristics can be identified as lack of focus, inability to give short- to long-term attention, hyperactivity in speech and body language, impulsive behaviors that can result in low self-esteem, and problems interacting with other people around the individual.

Culture Shock
This has very heavy similarities to PSAD in the sense that it is a disorientation and/or confusion for the individual as the result of changing his or her lifestyle, location, people he or she associates with, daily patterns, and habits. Culture shock is more of a sociological issue given that it is caused more from an individual's surroundings

Insomnia
Insomnia is the inability to sleep or to allow the mind and body to completely shut down. Due to the lack of achieving REM sleep state, the mind and body never fully recover from day-to-day activities. Therefore, the individual's body may undergo massive fatigue or overload, and on occasion, the mind can begin to go delusional.

Addiction

Addiction can be defined as the complete enslavement of the mind and body to a substance, behavior, and/or emotion and can have crash or withdrawal effects. It is the inability to deny the body's want or need for any one or multiple different vices that have proven to do more harm than good to the individual. There is no longer control within the individual's body or mind to deny the gratification that comes from feeding the body with said vice or vices.

Obsessive-Compulsive Disorder (OCD)

For any individual suffering from Obsessive-Compulsive Disorder (OCD), the need to do certain things over and over can help alleviate the heavy burden of obsession, for example, excessive shopping, the need to clean something by scrubbing it for hours, and/or odd behavior that has massive repetition.

It all Starts with PSAD?

Take note. Some of the behaviors and symptoms that have been illustrated throughout this book in regard to PSAD can easily match the criterion for any of these mental illnesses, yet not one time was there ever mentioned experiencing or witnessing combat, traumatic experiences, and/or intense situations (with exception to PTSD). Add to that, for most veterans, a lot of the mental illnesses come to life *after* they come home from active service. Therefore, it is possible to conclude that the mental illnesses the veteran is experiencing are a by-product of PSAD.

Think of it in another light. A veteran who was honorably discharged from service could not have been suffering these ailments at that present moment of active service; otherwise his or her command or superiors would have designated him or her a medical risk. Yes, there is a possibility that mental illnesses were probably there in a subconscious state, but why is it that transitioning to civilian world seems to be the culprit in aggravating so many issues? Could it be simply because that young adult who joined the military was sent down a different path of training, discipline, and internal growth and culture that does not conjoin with civilian life in any regard? Perhaps it could it be concluded that the sudden transition, with little to no preparation to civilian culture is the root of the tension and problems that bubble to the surface for so many thousands of veterans.

PSAD

OTHER POSSIBLE VARIABLES OF PSAD

Cops or Criminals

BASED ON OUTSIDE OBSERVATION and maintaining contact with Marines I served with, it is fair to say that a lot of Infantryman and military personnel usually become police officers. A high level of camaraderie and military field tactics are very similar and utilized by today's law enforcement personnel. However, this still does not aid the veteran nor law enforcement workers in coping with his or her personal needs in a civilian world. Divorce, stress-coping skills, alcoholism, and an understanding of civilian etiquette are all factors that even police officers deal with on a daily basis.

For those who do not enter law enforcement, other various forms of aggressive labor jobs are a good match for Marines entering civilian life, such as construction and oil field. However, due to personal struggles and many ailments listed earlier in this text, breaking the law can become a new challenge for veterans. Speeding tickets, DUI/DWI, possession of a controlled substance, theft, assault, and domestic abuse are all common issues that service members can accumulate as a result of suffering from adjustment issues.

In either case, becoming a police officer or a criminal are both examples of living a very aggressive lifestyle. They are just at opposite ends of the spectrum.

Wasting Educational Benefits

The government uses benefits like the GI Bill to entice civilians to join the military, but due to many personal problems, several veterans are not or cannot complete their degree plans. From personal experience and observing many other veterans, service members are coming home and, on many occasions, beginning the process of looking for a higher education as a means to move their lives to the next step. They will then tap into their educational benefits.

However, after the stressors of civilian transition begin to take place, dropout rates start to grow at an astronomical rate. In theory, it is possible to conclude that this is causing a massive financial hemorrhage for both the American taxpayers and veterans.

I personally know of several veterans who, upon returning home from service, enrolled in college just for the paycheck. The mentality behind that is that college should be easier to handle than the military, and it buys the veteran some more transitional time to figure out his or her next move. Whether the veteran is ready for school or not does not matter and a lot of times, the individual rarely knows what degree he or she wants to pursue. Furthermore, if he or she passes or fails is irrelevant. Bottom line— the veteran just needs the paycheck to stay afloat.

 SOLUTIONS

Awareness! Awareness! Awareness!

LIKE OTHER AILMENTS AND mental illnesses, awareness (by all parties) is key to identifying the existence of the problem and the first of many steps toward a solution. There is plenty of room for growth in a therapeutic capacity on all levels to include but not limited to the following: the general public, psychologists, social workers, counselors, schools, teachers, law enforcement, employers, friends, family members, and, of course, the veterans themselves.

It may sound complicated, but with a little organization and methodical planning, I truly believe that this problem of PSAD can be addressed if multiple entities are involved. Obviously, the ultimate goal is to help military personnel transition back to their civilian settings with greater ease and brighter futures than the struggles that are currently plaguing so many.

First, we cannot and must not mess with any current military Standard Operating Procedures (S.O.P.) or time frames. Our current Secretary of Defense General Mattis, said it best, "We need to have our men and women of the Armed Forces at the highest level of mission readiness as possible." I am in complete agreement with that. Aside from that, there are many other areas of ideal immediate growth for PSAD that could directly impact veterans for the better.

To start, research must be developed and conducted to obtain a much clearer interpretation and understanding of PSAD. In the world of psychology and social work, therapy programs need to be modified and created to cater directly toward adjustment issues. Schools can train their teachers and staff to become aware of possible signs and triggers of PSAD for veterans that are in their classes. They can then get the schools more involved with proper aid. Employers can train their management staff to watch for signs of possible struggles the veteran is going through. Immediate family members can attend a few classes when their veteran comes home so that they are better prepared as to what to expect. All of these suggestions are relatively simple and with methodical planning and organizing, I truly feel we can turn this around in a positive direction. By doing so, perhaps we can help veterans become better citizens by attending the right therapy classes and receiving proper guidance instead of being sent to prison, ending up homeless, or killing themselves.

A Critical Window

Based on my experience and after many discussions with veterans and social workers over the years, I can honestly conclude that there is a critical window that occurs within the first five years of discharge from active duty. These crucial years can be the determining factor in the success or failure of the transition process for many veterans. This, in my opinion, would be the ideal time in a veteran's life to mentally prepare and plan for the dramatic transition and adjustment he or she will face upon discharge. Classes and transitional programs need to be in place to aid all veterans within or around those years.

The Department of Defense's Transitional Readiness Program (TRP) is or should be designated as the first line of defense in beginning to raise awareness amongst soon-to-be veterans of the problems associated with PSAD. Someone needs to make an actual appearance at these TRP classes in order to make the future veterans aware of possible obstacles they will face once they reach the civilian world, and a seven- to ten-day class is not sufficient. The future veterans need to understand the differences between themselves and civilians and how those differences can possibly affect their future.

Finances

Finances are another great place to begin changing the way veterans adjust to civilian life. There is actually a pretty simple option for consideration. It goes as follows.

A civilian young adult going through those trials and errors during the same age range as his or her military counterpart is usually spending about 40 or 45 percent of his or her net pay per month, give or take, on basic living expenses. Obviously this number fluctuates based on many variables such as financial discipline, responsibility, spending habits, and job pay. No matter the case, that civilian individual has to designate a certain amount of money per paycheck for rent, utilities, grocery money, and all other living expenses. If he or she does not pay these basic bills, then there are severe consequences, for example, eviction, disconnection of utilities, and/or vehicle repossession. Whatever is left over is what would be considered disposable income and can be spent on whatever that person chooses.

A very similar financial plan can be offered to service members as an option. After making service members aware of the financial adjustment dangers they may face upon discharge, they can option in and choose from different financial packages with different investment levels. They then will physically go to their financial institution, withdraw money on every payday, and then deposit into said plan—no automatic withdrawal!

The main purpose of the financial plan is to engrain in the service member the importance of limiting spending, saving money for the future, as well as getting used to having half of his or her paycheck going to bills. These financial plans can be set up as money is deposited from the service member into an account, it accumulates a nice healthy return for when the service member discharges. If the service member does not comply with the obligations set forth by the financial plan, then penalties are given—just like a civilian would go through if he or she did not pay their monthly bills.

I would highly recommend that this be given as an option simply because no one likes to be forced what to do with their own money. Those who do lock themselves into the financial plan are going to hate the penalties, but that is supposed to happen. A civilian the same age as the service member is learning the harsh truths about money management outside the military, and those lessons will carry them for the rest of their lives. The same needs to happen to service members. If they do not stick to their bills, they will face severe consequences and can possibly wind up becoming another homeless statistic.

This is merely a suggestion. Financial strategies need to be assessed and researched so the lesson is learned for the service member while not interfering with military training and combat readiness.

Modify and/or Amend Current VA Benefits

By instilling a new transitional benefit upon release of service, a monitoring program can be developed to help aid veterans as they come home. Veterans can choose to participate in a short to long-term VA transitional program that offers some form of compensation in turn for allowing a VA officer to closely monitor all aspects of the veteran's daily life.

How is the job search going? Has the veteran found a good home? Is there help needed with schoolwork or study habits? How are things going with family and friends? Does anything feel weird or out of place? Finally, and most importantly, does he or she need anything?

The enticement for veterans would be a financial draw, job leads, and/or good housing. Currently many rehabilitation programs offer these exact benefits—only they are mostly offered *after* a veteran is already hurting with problems. Let's offer these benefits before the downward spiral begins.

A Big Brother/Sister Program

There are plenty of veterans who have already been home for a number of years, and perhaps a new incentive program can be developed in which senior veterans can aid junior veterans. Through the VA or other outside resources, any individual veteran who has successfully transitioned to the civilian world can technically become a mentor to any service member who has just been released. Through proper screening procedures, the VA can compensate veterans who take on new veterans to show them what to expect and the ins and outs of becoming a civilian again. Veterans listen to other veterans, and something like this can become a great asset to both veterans and the VA.

A Suggested Curriculum

The following curriculum is merely a suggestion to directly attack and address employment and financial problems that many veterans will face almost immediately upon discharge.

I strongly suggest that an additional six months be added to every military contract out there. During this period, there will be _no_ formations or military obligations of any kind. Instead, these six months offer a service member a much-needed buffer period to properly adjust and allow time to get benefits and resources in full working order.

Currently in the United States, the time frame it takes, in most cases, for any individual to obtain his or her first paycheck from a solid, gainful, steady job can be anywhere from six months to a year. That does not include any complications that can occur along the way. The days of shaking someone's hand and handing in an application and a smile are over. The order of operation for obtaining gainful employment usually is as follows: job searches, applications, building and perfecting résumés, first interview and then the second, background check, orientation, and training. All of that takes a very long time before anyone can get a solid paycheck he or she can count on.

Those extra six months would help the service member overcome any financial obstacles as he or she would still be receiving military pay. By simply adding six months to every contract, we offer a veteran a better chance at a smoother transition that, in my opinion, is very well deserved.

Another critical need during this six-month transitional time on contract would be classes—civilian classes to be exact. One thing that a military person should be very familiar with is training, and adding a civilian training course to those six months of his or her contract can prepare him or her immensely for the road ahead. The old saying that "piss-poor preparation leads to piss-poor performance" is a clear sign that a need for civilian training should be developed for outgoing service members.

Management personnel from human resource departments of "we support our troops" companies can come out to some of these classes and speak to new veterans directly. This would be a great opportunity for these companies to both learn from service members as well as teach them the SOPs of their companies. An incentive of a tax break can be created for these companies to create a draw and make that extra effort to help our veterans.

Social workers who have helped struggling veterans in addition to veterans who have already gone through their own struggles can also be great teaching assets for outgoing military personnel. The cool thing about that is that you can have veterans speak and give testimonies to their own particular branches of military, and nothing drives the point home further than someone who's already been through it.

CONCLUSION

WHENEVER A VETERAN GOES off the deep end or takes his or her own life, the biggest question on everyone's mind is, "Why?" The main objective of this book is to start answering that question and to introduce the concept of PSAD. It was a basic step-by-step process as to how a person goes from young adult enlistee in the Armed Forces to a completely broken-down American who served his or her country. It was also meant to draw a generic map as to how a person can join the military, receive an Honorable Discharge, and then wind up in a catastrophic state with so many problems, such as homelessness, addiction, criminal activity, and/or suicidal.

Based on this text, it is fair to say that the catalyst that is wreaking so much havoc on veterans is _adjustment_ to civilian life after serving. Think of it in another way. The civilian is taken out, and the Marine/Sailor/Soldier/Airman is extensively trained and put in at the beginning of service. Well, how do we take the service member out and put the civilian _back_ when he or she is done with his or her contract?

At the present moment, service members are released from service and flung back into the sea of civilian world. And then they are expected to have the tools to survive on their own. In reality, they do have many great tools—only they are meant for the military world and have no place in a civilian setting. We as a country are failing our military on all sides in helping service personnel transition back to civilian world. PTSD, bipolar, ADHD, chemical dependency, and all other mental illnesses may be present in the veteran, but, in my opinion, can be aggravated from the start by PSAD.

The good news, in my opinion, is that we can fix this or at least make a dramatic impact of change. A lot of work is required before we can understand the problem fully. Research must be conducted in order to prove this concept is real. Solutions and therapy programs need to be developed that are dialed in more to helping veterans with adjustment issues.

This concept of PSAD is in its infancy stages, and the only way for this to gain traction is to hear your stories. If you fell apart when you came home or are struggling to readjust to civilian life, I politely ask you to think about what was the biggest part you struggled with.

My goal is to have the entire country thinking about this, and I want to hear your feedback. Once again, this is just a basic map of how things can fall apart for a veteran.

If you are a veteran and can identify with any of this, then submit your input. If you are a civilian and have witnessed this in a veteran, you also have an opportunity to submit your input. Let's start working together and help our military and our veterans come home properly.

If you would like to submit any reflection, testimony or suggestions, I gladly welcome it. Please send it to: input@psad03.com

This concept needs momentum and every little bit helps. I thank you for taking the time to read this and for helping to fight the good fight!!

2nd Battalion, 1st Marines, Echo Co. 3rd Platoon
15th Marine Expeditionary Unit
1997–2001

Members of 3rd Platoon

Beau Briggs, Allen Smith, Alfons Kunze, James Haslip, Harold Cruz, Luis Camarena, Jeremiah Herrera, Josue Magana, Daniel Valdez, Matt Hoyt, Kris Nicholson, Seth Menard, Howard DeLaCruz, Kevin Allen Johnson, Louis Wolcott, Sean McGrew, Jeff Walding, Oscar Nowell, Saul Avila, Eric Haughey, Cody IronCloud, Jason Whalen, Patrick Morgan, Ryan Moran, P.J. Espinoza, Reynaldo Rios, Jarred Dubois Timothy Wayne Shaw, Christof Walti, Enrique Zambrano, Gerald Noe, Andrew McAllister, Alex Solorio, Juan Salazar, Marcus Santiago, Dan Shirey, Robert Hetrick, Robert Aldrich, Seth Adkerson, Chris Ray, Phillip "Doc" Lucero, Sgt. Olguin, Steve Szymceck, Don Travis, Peter Best

Other Members of 2nd Battalion, 1st Marines,
1st Marine Regiment (1997–2001):

Christopher Mike Musquiz, Marc Montez, Seth Carlson, Jason Alexander, Ryan Kendrick, Raymond Lopez, Mort Scales, Daniel Sword, Israel Gettinger, Louis Gallardo, Benjamin Rowella, Todd

Hubbard, Pete Jimenez, Joseph Born, Jeff Bowen, Jose A. Tirado, Jose Marquez, Jason Cherne, Rick Worden, Bryan Hayes, Gabe DeLeon, Vladimir Pichugin, Derrick Allison, Eric Comer, Chuck Throckmorton, William Bishop, Darren Malchow, Garrett Miller, Ruben Amezcua, Heviter Saul Paraiso, Brad Leonard, Danny Rosa, Chris Wright, Kyle Fiori, Armando Hueso, Thomas Chase, Manuel GarciaLeon, Clinton Fields, Maurizio Alfaro, John Ploskanka, Junior Hernandez, William Huang, Jim Smith, Patrick Wallin, Justin Malesich, Christopher Covington, Shane Snyder, Andrew Larson, John C. McKinney II, Robert Wagner, Juan Sanchez, Ray Mendoza, Josh Goss, Isadore Bilbrew Jr., Scott Charlton, Andrew Bollinger, Gabriel Morales, Justin Holder, Eric Mendoza, Dan Leensvaart, Mario Alamillo, Reyes Gutierrez III, Salvador Parada, Ben Watson, Jimmie Sparks, Larry Watson, Scott Hasselback, Mario Aspiranti, John Cardozo, Christopher Banker, Harold Agurto, Jose Alicea III, Jason Billingsley, Roberto Cintora, Jake Atkinson, Joff Hall, Chad Murphy, Tony Jefferson, Robert Gregory Hyatt Jr., Nelson Campos, Armado Lopez, Chris Litton, Jason Arnt, James Erwin, Mark Manville, Fred Young, Joel Pendarvis, Brad Loudon, David Felix, Joe O'Connor, Raymond "Doc" Davis, John Ramirez, Vince Peralta Jr., Elmer Peraza, Jesse Ortiz, Patrick Keepers, Troy Abbott, Lonnie Johnson, David Schlumpburger, Cody Wyatt, Jon Schaffner, Brent Greene, Chris Kelner, Derek Mulvihill, Chris Holden, James Geiger, William Heath Holcomb, Aaron Kaminski, Nicholas Cottrell, Joseph "Doc" Padilla, Bryan "Doc" Rogers, Mark Carlton, David Benitez, Sean Bass, Nathan Fugate, Dustin Dacus, Steve Foolbear, Matthew Getz, Wesley Clingman, Brian McBrayer, Kevin G. Nave, Alex Echeverria, Andy Jensen, Tony Sanford, Courtney Anderson, James Van Duren, Rolf Howard, Michael Griffin, Staff Sgt. O'Laughlin, Gunnery Sgt. Hovey, Gunnery Sgt. Dixon, Lt. Getz, Lt. Staten, and Lt. Clinton

PALS

ABOUT THE AUTHOR

My Fight with PSAD

I was born and raised in San Antonio, Texas, to a hardworking mother and father. My father was a telecommunication engineer for a number of years, a small business owner, and a math teacher for middle-school students. His incredible business savvy carried him through some pretty successful investments over the years, and currently he is a real estate agent in the San Antonio area. My mother was the owner and operator of Sunset Mexican Restaurant, a family business in the San Antonio area for twenty-two years. As a second business venture, she opened her own reprographic business in San Antonio and ran it for over ten years before slowing things down and recently began working on her retirement. My older brother is a graduate from Texas A&M with a Master's in Business and became a Captain in the United States Marine Corps. He currently lives in Connecticut raising three beautiful little girls. To salute him was kinda weird, but we had fun with it over the Christmas Holidays. My younger brother is a high-level network technician for the cable company and has worked hard to make a name for himself from the ground up. His attention to detail, strong work ethic and ability to be so easygoing with people has enabled him to develop a good home and a great career. Our family has had its ups and downs, but we still have managed to make it work in one way or another.

High school was kind of a joke for me, considering I spent most of my time cutting class and getting into trouble. I found a new direction in the Marine Corps that I truly felt gave me all I needed to handle a great life. I did exceptionally well in boot camp and was meritoriously promoted upon graduation. I was then sent to the Infantry fleet with the 2nd Battalion, 1st Marines, Echo Co. 3rd Platoon, Camp Horno, Camp Pendleton, California, in 1997. We had a pretty tight unit of hardworking, motivated Devil Dogs and I'm thankful to have maintained close contact with a good majority of them through social media and reunions over the years. A lot of us have not seen each other in over ten years, yet the jokes and old times are always talked about like they just happened yesterday. As a former Marine, it really is a breath of fresh air to laugh at a bunch of disgustingly funny assholes who don't get their panties in a wad over the little things-- even if it is through a computer.

Like all Infantry Battalions, we had our fair share of troubled Marines, but for the most part, we were a great unit. My first deployment overseas was on the USS Harpers Ferry, USS Boxer, and USS Cleveland in 1998–1999 with the 15th Marine Expeditionary Unit. We had toured all through the Middle East and down the east coast of Africa before heading back stateside. Things took a crazy turn for me on our second deployment, however, due to a broken femur and clavicle.

I had never really seen myself as a "lifer"/twenty-year Marine, so as my contract was winding down, I began making preparations for my arrival back home in San Antonio. I had set up several job interviews, had lined up a good place to call home, and had a nice little chunky savings account, so things were looking pretty good. I was honorably discharged as a noncommissioned officer (NCO) (Corporal) in August of 2001.

When 9-11 happened, a lot of guys I served with had their contracts extended, but I was already home by then. My contract had ended roughly three weeks prior to when the Twin Towers were hit. I wanted to get back in to help, but my circumstances made it kind of hard to reenlist. I would have had to get a bunch of waivers and medical clearances to go back, so unfortunately, I had to watch everything happen from the outside. I came to grips with the fact that my life in the military was over and it was time to move on to the next chapter of my life.

I was quite excited to get back to San Antonio, and I was looking forward to building a family and a home. Unfortunately, all the preparations I had made did not go the way I had planned. I began to endure quite a number of setbacks due to failed business ventures and my own subconscious disorientation. Frequent heated debates with family and friends over petty differences on both my part and theirs started to get under my skin and aggravate the heck out of me. I had found a great girl who made me very happy, but given all the troubles I was enduring, my relationship with her ended on a very bad note.

Life got unexpectedly worse rather quickly as time progressed. My savings account was drained within a matter of a few months or so. I smashed my truck running into a deer on the highway, and things were getting pretty rough with my friends and social life as well. I went to work as head security at the local nightclub scene to help subsidize my income, but it still wasn't enough. I worked my way up from door security at a local pub to floor manager at a couple of strip clubs in the San Antonio area. My life became about sex, drugs, and rock and roll, literally and in retrospect, that line of work actually made things worse.

Within a couple of years, my world began to crumble all around me. Since I was pretty active in the bar scene, I started partying pretty aggressively and dabbling with hard drugs and alcohol. The downward spiral was a brutal, horrible time filled with confusion, broken promises (mostly on my part), and a development of some very bad habits. Over the next three to four years, life got to a point of total chaos. I had a hard time with jobs, social relationships, and financial stability, and soon enough, criminal activity began to cause even bigger problems for me.

I kept hearing people around me tell me that I was too loud, too amped up, too aggressive, too passionate, too extreme, undisciplined, and irresponsible. (Those last two would really upset me the most.) I was annoying and rough around the edges. You name it. Simply put, the world around me did not understand me, and I did not understand it.

My first rock bottom came in early 2006, almost five years after discharge. It really was inevitable given my involvement in such radical, self-destructive behavior. I was stranded in a very bad part of San Antonio on a Sunday morning with not a dime to my name. I had lost my girl, my truck, my home, and my life. The depression was pretty brutal, and the shame of losing my life in such a bad way was pretty overbearing. I wanted to crawl into a hole and die. I could not bear the thought that I was a "weak" individual and needed help. In a lot of ways, that is what made admitting I had so many problems so hard to do. I had hung with the best in the Marines, and I was part of something that less than 3 percent of the world could do. Yet something as simple as living a civilian life was incredibly difficult for me. It made absolutely no sense to me at all. I was broken. I was hollowed out. I was dying inside...

I was admitted into a few inpatient treatment and rehabilitation programs that year. I had some good inspiration from my parents and found a drive to learn as much as I possibly could to get out of that mess. I guess you can say that was where I first started learning all about mental health issues and psychosocial therapies. It was interesting how, even in my darkest hours, life was trying to teach me things that I could use later in life to help people around me. It was a very bumpy road, and I spent the next two to three years struggling to attain a gainful therapy program with plagued relapses and letdowns along the way.

One of the biggest challenges for me was that there were many times that I truly felt hopeless and worthless at the same time. The biggest question that continually baffled me was: how the hell did

I come from a Corporal in the Marine Corps to a homeless addict in a matter of a few years? There were no answers to my questions. Furthermore, I had to endure a lot of ridicule and abandonment from my closest friends. To be honest, I had done my fair share of letting them down; therefore, that only added more guilt to my already troubled mind. When I would sit in front of someone close to me or a professional therapist, I was met with a lot of pity that I did not want and was dealt with in a very elementary way that made me feel even more like a loser.

There were a lot of people telling me over and over, "You need to do this," or, "You need to do that." Everyone around me seemed to have it all figured out and, in their mind, had all the answers for me. It would infuriate me to no end. I was trying. I *really* was. I was trying anything and everything to make sense of all the mess in my life and get things back in order. Unfortunately, the harder I tried, the darker my world would get.

It was in 2007 and my third consecutive hard attempt at recovery that things started looking up. When that happened, I was in pretty rough shape. My body had a vicious chemical odor coming out of it, and I was very, very sick. I finally surrendered that I was in a really bad spot. It no longer mattered to me how bad the embarrassment was or how I looked to other people. I had to accept and surrender to a very hard truth. If I could not resolve the runaway freight train of adjustment problems I had first, then everything after that—that is, a job or a family—would never have a chance of success. Bottom line, I just wanted the bad times to end. Period. And I could not for the life of me get them to end on my own.

Finally, after many years of despair and pain, I surrendered. One hundred percent complete and total mental and Spiritual surrender. I embraced humility and stopped denying my own defeat. I stopped fighting and arguing with everybody and everything. I stopped trying to convince myself that I'm tough and can figure it out on my own. I shut my mouth, opened my ears, and began to really listen.

The VA

In my opinion, the VA gets way too much of a bad rap. Yes, there have been many cases of bad situations, neglected veterans, accidental oversights, and atrocious horror stories of bad VA procedures and personnel. But unfortunately, those bad stories *grossly* overshadow a lot of really good doctors, therapists, nurses, social workers, administrators and specialists who really do care a lot about what they do. It's the classic case of how a thousand good things are done right and everyone looks at the one bad thing that was done wrong. It is of my opinion, that for every one bad thing you hear in the VA, thousands of really good things happen every day that will never see the light of day.

These doctors and therapists taught me a lot about the conscious and subconscious mind—how the brain processes and struggles with trauma, especially in regards to Freeze, Fight or Flight syndrome. I learned the path that drugs and alcohol take as they are ingested into the body. I learned how the chemicals affect the dopamine and serotonin levels of the brain and the very core of the disease of addiction. I learned a lot about the reptilian brain, the emotional brain, and the logical brain or the cortex, along with all of the various forms of social therapies that help unravel the onion of layers of problems each individual can accumulate.

There is no doubt in my mind or heart that, if not for these social workers who give so much of themselves, my recovery would never have come to fruition. I have had the great fortune to meet a great team of recovery specialists who patiently taught me the basics of psychosocial therapies almost ten years ago and have stayed by me even to this day. They constantly open their door to help me and thousands of veterans with the daily struggles of life, and that level of care is absolutely priceless. Oftentimes, I'm completely baffled how some of these social workers can sit and listen to so many broken veterans and their stories every single day of the week over and over again for years and years.

I learned a great deal about Dialectical Behavioral Therapy from one of the most brilliant brain experts I have ever known, and I admire her incredible ability to make it make sense and interesting in layman's terms. She has a great knack for being compassionate and understanding while at the same time calling me out on my bullshit. I've had a substance abuse therapist who is always on standby when I need him the most and is a phone call away. He will always find time for me to come in and talk things out. Our conversations over the years have really helped me to obtain such an incredible grasp on the basic field of psychology. He's been in the field of veteran therapy for over thirty years, and when I presented this theory/concept of PSAD to him, his encouragement kept me going. All of these resources are at my disposal due to the expert leadership of a great director at this VA facility. He could have very easily told me, "We've done enough for you; you're on your own." Yet he never has. His understanding of veterans and their daily struggles enables him to embrace and encourage the importance of strong aftercare.

Slow, Steady Progression

Unfortunately, I was never able to shake the pity and ridicule from friends and family around me. I had to learn the harsh truth that I was not the only one that suffered when I came home. Someone close to me once told me that I had to learn patience on top of figuring out how to get my life back together. I was in such a rush to try to save face and make things right with people I had hurt that I failed to focus more on obtaining long-term recovery so the tornado of relapse would not spawn again. A lot of good friends and family got trampled along the way by the self-destructive behaviors of my bad times. I had worked as hard as I could to rebuild relationships, and many people, including my brothers, did all they could to stick by me. However, there was a lot of irreparable damage with old girlfriends, childhood friends, and even some family members.

Things were definitely in a state of hot and cold for the next couple of years. However, I was able to get a solid foot on recovery in 2009 given that I never stopped going to recovery classes and Faith-based retreats. Since I was having a very difficult time finding long term employment, I found a proactive outlet by getting involved in a lot of volunteer work. I learned that the best place to aid in getting my life together was to get out of myself and help other people around me. Volunteering like that taught me to not think of the life I wanted, but rather to be thankful for the life I already have. The best lesson in humility I learned was that there is *always* someone in a darker place than I and that I could help him or her in one way or another.

As time progressed in the oil field/construction world, something started to make me feel a little strange. I was totally content on the rebuilding that was happening, yet a yearning began to grow inside my heart. While I was on the downtime, between jobs, I continued very heavily in volunteer work, giving personal testimonies and motivational talks and getting involved in group discussions. A truly amazing thing began to take shape.

When my life had fallen apart the way it did, when I was discharged from active duty, I truly felt as if the bad choices I had made were totally against the core values that had been instilled in me from the Marine Corps. The hardest thing that made absolutely no sense was that I was not some lazy sack of shit who enjoyed mooching off everyone. Yet that was exactly where I was. I was a hard worker who could not hold a job. I absolutely loved to socialize, yet fitting back into civilian relationships and civilian settings felt odd and uncomfortable to me. I was a motivated, smart, go-getter who had trouble every month following through with my obligations. I was entitled to many Veteran benefits, yet, I was homeless and broke all the time with no direction or hope for the future.

The shame and embarrassment that came with that way of life made me feel very isolated and alone. On top of that, I thought I was the only one that was going through falling apart like that. However, after getting involved and listening to a lot of other veterans, I began to learn that thousands of people were experiencing the same thing in one way or another.

Not the Only One

In April of 2012, a Marine brother I served my full four years with took his own life. As word began to circulate about what had happened to him, I could not believe what I was hearing. The hard times he had endured were a little different yet very similar to mine, and it took him to the point of suicide. It was a very clear sign that this problem for veterans was very real and not just some isolated case.

By staying in constant communication with fellow veterans I have met through the years, along with my own unit of Marines through social-media outlets, I have observed a pattern emerge. There are quite a lot of former service members who cannot stay sober, keep a good home together, stay out of trouble, and maintain a strong, healthy lifestyle. I personally know and served with a large number of these men and women. They are hardworking, dedicated, and motivated, squared away individuals who did not deserve the hardships they endured and still endure today.

It is my opinion, Post-Service Adjustment Disorder (PSAD) affects all veterans—only on different levels. Some veterans manage to struggle a little and then get things back on track. Others can blend into civilian culture right away, only to have PSAD bubble to the surface in later years. The biggest heartache is that there are hundreds of thousands of veterans who go all the way off the deep end in one form or another after discharge. If you don't believe me, go to your local VA hospital and ask them about their inpatient mental health/rehabilitation programs. Every one I've ever encountered, called, or researched has a waiting list of veterans looking for a bed and/or needing help.

In closing, I would like to say once again, that the good news is that I truly believe PSAD is something we can fix. What needs to be considered is how to stop the veteran before he or she starts a fire in their life and burns down all that was accomplished in the military to the ground. We have to accept our own humility and look in the mirror to find out our own individual parts in all of this. Then we must find the guts to do something about it the right way....... in a healthy way.

Printed in the United States
By Bookmasters